...But Seriously, Folks!

more cartoons by Pat Oliphant

Foreword by Studs Terkel

Andrews and McMeel, Inc.
A Universal Press Syndicate Company
Kansas City • New York

Foreword

Regard the Oliphant of May 6, 1983:

Ronnie, our prez, the Great American Toby, with arms crossed, Shiva style, points at opposite panels, each featuring an armed Latino. At the one marked El Salvador, our laughing boy says: "Foreign policy is a snap — all you have to remember is Communist guerrilla . . . here" — as his other index finger indicates the opposite panel marked Nicaragua — "and Freedom Fighter . . . here." The soldiers are identical. Almost lost, yet definitely present, is the ubiquitous tiny penguin in the lower corner. It is the cartoonist's Greek chorus chirping, "I'm glad to have that cleared up."

It is vintage Oliphant. It makes mincemeat of Jeane Kirkpatrick's dragon lady latherings and William Buckley's tortuous polysyllables. It is the hallmark of the gimlet-eyed political cartoonist from Daumier to now.

Considering the mildness of the man's personal demeanor, the weaponry of Pat Oliphant is astonishingly lethal. As Hemingway once said of the Chicago writer Algren, "He hits with both fists. If you don't watch out, he'll kill you" — so you are herewith warned of Oliphant. With one felt pen, he devastates. His targets have always been worthy of his sketched-out scorn: the banally powerful and their assorted lickspittles, official and unofficial, here, there, everywhere.

Of course, he draws a bead on the Russian Bear, the Ayatollah, the Libyan wild man, and their likes; but that's par for the course even for the no-balls, nongifted ones. Those are the baddies out *there*. Pat Oliphant, in the tradition of the great ones, is at his best much closer to home. When he takes aim at Laughing Boy, the incredible Watt, Cap the Knife, and our freedom-loving allies, Begin and the Central American colonels, let alone our Chilean creatures, he is Joe Louis in action. He wastes no punches; but when he delivers — wham! And you know there's more where that came from.

I was unaware of his work as a young Aussie cartoonist in the port city, Adelaide. Some sharp-eyed editor in the Rockies knew something the rest of us didn't know when he brought him in 1964 to the *Denver Post* as a replacement for the formidable Conrad. Since that day, a fortunate one for us, Pat Oliphant has worked, effortlessly, into the American muckraking tradition. Not quite. The influence of the British David Low is there as well as of Vicky, the Middle European refugee. Yet, it is the distinctive touch of Thomas Aloysius Dorgan (Tad) that is most apparent. He did his stuff in the early twenties on the sports pages of the Hearst papers. At least, that's where I saw his cartoons.

I remember, as a kid, immediately after studying the baseball box scores, turning toward Tad. I was taken with those tiny creatures, usually cats, in the corner of the panel. Their commentaries were casually trenchant, uncannily like those of Oliphant's penguins. What makes this remarkable is that the young Australian had never seen any of Tad's work.

Consider the Oliphant of July 28, 1982:

Laughing Boy, Secretary Schultz and a death's head in junta uniform are peering into a mass grave near the wall marked El Salvador. The caption reads: "Ah, not too many, at all! That shows a distinct improvement in human rights, Mr. Schultz." At the bottom of the right hand corner are two tiny creatures. One chirps, "'E' for effort." The other says, "'D' for dead."

Stephen Becker, in his excellent work, *Comic Art in America,* says of Dorgan: "With the keen nose of a man who had seen fights dumped and horse races fixed, he sniffed out the phony. . . . He was a toughie." So it is today; in far more deadly matters, Pat Oliphant spots the marked cards and the rigged ball game. And loony self-righteousness. And three-dollar-bill piousness.

If there is a definitive example of Pat Oliphant's hitting the bull's eye, it's in his work of March 16, 1983:

There are two nuclear weapons poised at the heavens. One sports the Stars and Stripes. On it, we read: "This is a righteous, decent, pious, God-blessed, psalm-singing, peace-loving, church-going, Christian nuclear weapon." The other sports the hammer and sickle. On it, we read: "This is a truly evil, nonbelieving, no-good, war-mongering, Communist, atheist nuclear weapon." Down below, in between the missiles, is Europe.

A tiny man says to a tiny woman: "What a comfort to be on the side of the angels." Anyone who has been knocked out by Mark Twain's "War Prayer" will recognize a kindred spirit here.

Turn these pages and see if you don't agree.

STUDS TERKEL

'MENACHEM SENT ME.'

'SECOND THE MOTION!'

'HE WOULDN'T SIGN — HE SAYS THERE'S TOO MUCH REGULATION IN THE WORLD AS IT IS.'

THE CREATURE FROM THE LOVE CANAL

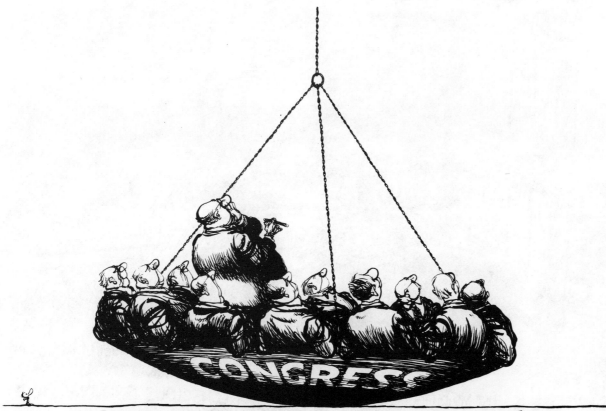

'ALL BALANCED AT THIS END, MR. PRESIDENT. HOW'S EVERYTHING AT YOUR END?'

July 22, 1982

'COME IN, MY DEAR. THIS IS JUST YOUR GOOD OLD ENVIRONMENTALLY CONSCIOUS GRANDMA, AND ANY RESEMBLANCE TO JAMES WATT IS PURELY COINCIDENTAL.'

'AH, NOT TOO MANY, AT ALL! THAT SHOWS A DISTINCT IMPROVEMENT IN HUMAN RIGHTS, MR. SCHULTZ.'

August 6, 1982

August 9, 1982

'I DON'T APPROVE OF THIS WHOLE ACT — YOU REMEMBER THAT!'

August 11, 1982

MR REAGAN WAS HOPING FOR A NICE PARAKEET...

THE NEW RIGHT

WAITING FOR REAGAN

August 12, 1982

"... AND HE SAID, 'DID YOU KNOW THAT EMBRACING THIS DEFICIT IS LIKE HOLDING YOUR NOSE AND HUGGING A PIG?' 'NOT,' I SAID, 'UNTIL YOU CAME ALONG, YOU SILVER-TONGUED OL' COMMUNICATOR, YOU.'"

'NO, WE DON'T WANT TO DISCUSS ABORTION WITH YOU — WE DON'T WANT TO DISCUSS ANYTHING WITH YOU, SENATOR HELMS!'

SUPER SALESMAN, TOUGH TOWN

"NO! NO! — BUY! BUY! NOT 'BYE-BYE!'"

ALL QUIET ON THE MID-EAST FRONT

August 26, 1982

"CLASS WILL CONFINE ITS STYLE OF CLASSROOM PRAYER TO THE NORMAL, PROPER, ACCEPTED, CONSERVATIVE, ALL-AMERICAN, RIGHT-WING CHRISTIAN VARIETY!"

September 2, 1982

September 8, 1982

'OK, CLOSE UP A LITTLE . . . OK, NOW ALL SMILE FOR THE ARAB UNITY PHOTO . . . '

September 10, 1982

THE OVER-RIDE

38

September 15, 1982

'PUT IT OUT — I THINK WE'RE STUCK WITH CURSING THE DARKNESS!'

'AGENT ORANGE? WE'RE STUDYING ON IT — WHAT MORE DO YOU WANT?'

STUDYING OUR OPTIONS ON THE BEIRUT MASSACRE.

'THE SOFT, SLANTING LIGHT OF AUTUMN. THE GENTLE, MELLOW AIR. FUNNY LITTLE COLORED THINGS FALLING OFF THE TREES. SUNDAY AFTERNOON. THERE'S NO FOOTBALL. I'M OUTSIDE! AAARGH!'

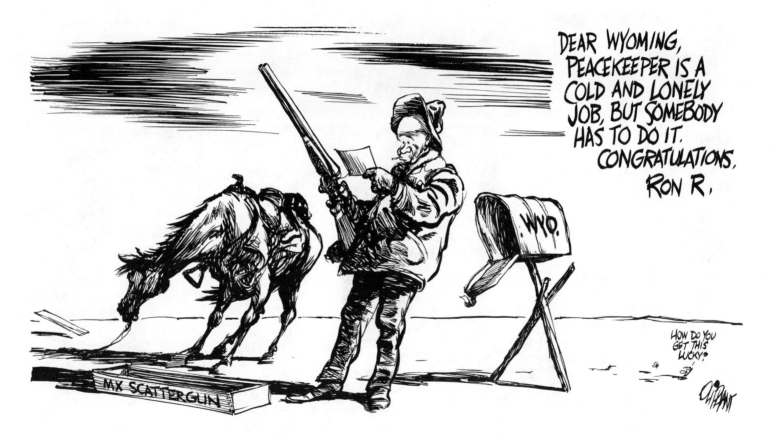

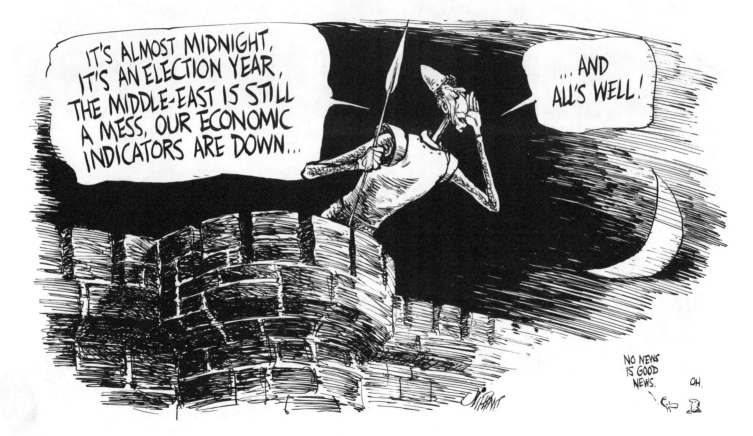

'HE'S EVEN TRIED PRAYER TO END THE NFL STRIKE. THANK YOU VERY MUCH FOR JAMMING HIS TRANSMISSIONS.'

October 1, 1982

'NEVER MIND THE WAR POWERS RESOLUTION, MY BOY — IF WE GET STUCK OUT THERE, CONGRESS WILL BUILD YOU A NICE MONUMENT.'

50

'NOW ASK THEM IF THEY HAVE EVER BEEN, AND WHY ARE THEY NOW, COMMUNIST, PINKO, SUBVERSIVES.'

October 7, 1982

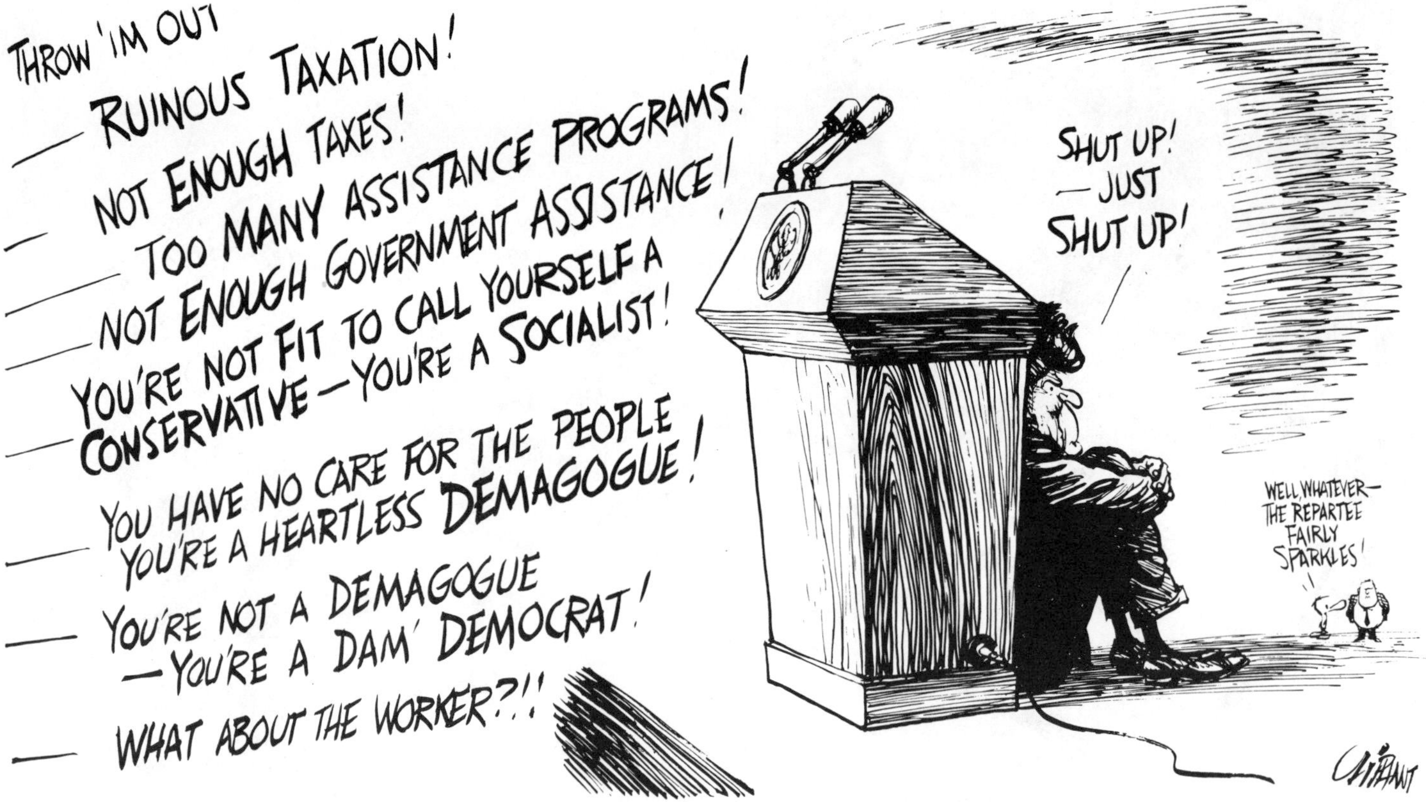

'CAP'N VOLCKER, MAY I BORROW THE PARACHUTE?'

'WHO'S INSIDE?'

October 13, 1982

THE NOT-SO-GOOD SAMARITAN

57

October 14, 1982

'THAT MUST BE WHAT HE MEANS BY "STAYING THE COURSE".'

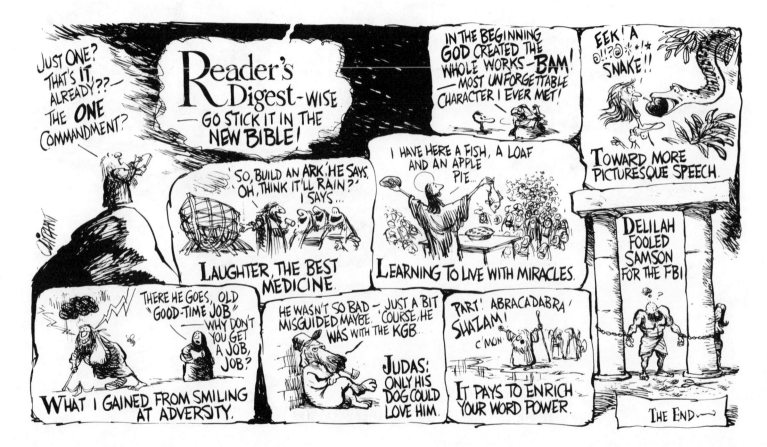

'MAKE UP YOUR MIND — WHERE DO YOU WANT THIS?'

'...THIS, HOWEVER, SHOULD NOT, IN ANY WAY, BE CONSTRUED AS A CHANGE OF ZOO POLICY.'

October 22, 1982

'A TABLE, IF YOU PLEASE, FAR FROM THE MADDING NOUVEAU BROKE.'

'YOU THINK IT'S CREEPY NOW, WAIT TILL WE COME BACK AFTER DARK.'

'I'VE ALREADY BEEN TRICKED.'

October 27, 1982

67

'EMMA V. CATHCART, ON SOCIAL SECURITY, IS NOW VOTING!'

LOSERS, 1982

November 4, 1982

72

'YOU'RE NOT HELPING ONE BIT, Y'KNOW...'

November 10, 1982

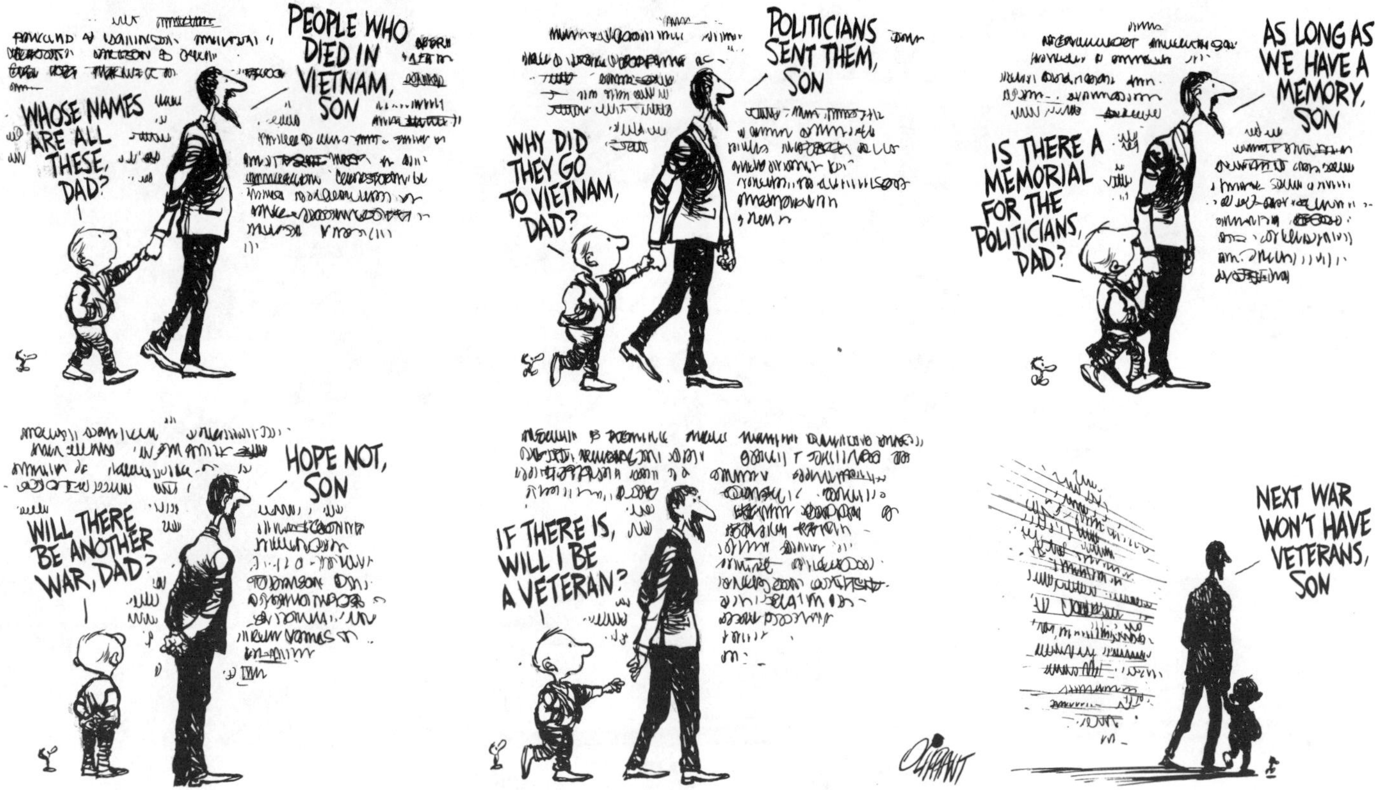

YOUR WIFE IS READY. LAST WEEK YOU INADVERTENTLY PROMISED TO GO WITH HER TO THE CIVIC PRESERVATION SOCIETY LECTURE, THIS SUNDAY AFTERNOON IN THE WOMEN'S CLUB AUDITORIUM. WHY, HERE SHE COMES NOW....

'OK, THAT'S GOOD — NOW, HOLD IT.'

November 20, 1982

THE CHINA CARD

79

GIVE THANKS. ATHLETICS RETURNS TO THE AMERICAN SCENE.

'IT DOESN'T MEAN A BITTER WINTER— BUT THERE IS AN EIGHTY PERCENT CHANCE YOU COULD GET DEVOURED BY BIG, HAIRY CATERPILLARS.'

'THIS IS YOUR CAPTAIN SPEAKING. WELCOME ABOARD EASTBOUND AIRLINES CUTRATE TRANSCONTINENTAL EIGHT DOLLAR ROUNDTRIP FLIGHT FROM LOS ANGELES TO NEW YORK...'

'HEY, LOOK WHO'S BACK! HOW WAS SOUTH AMERICA, MAN? YOU FIND ANY COUNTRY WOULD GIVE US A LOAN?'

December 6, 1982

86

THE SPIRIT OF PROTECTIONISM

December 9, 1982

'THE PUBLIC HAS GOTTEN THE IDEA THAT DENSE PACK IS A RUBE GOLDBERG.' — SEN. JACKSON

`I NEVER HEARD OF THE GHOST OF CHRISTMAS D.W.I. — AND WHAT ARE WE DOING HERE..?'

December 15, 1982

91

December 17, 1982

'LET ME TELL YOU FELLAS HOW IT WAS IN "HELLCATS OF THE NAVY"...'

WATCHDOG

'GIVE ME SOMETHING SWEET AND SENTIMENTAL FOR CHRISTMAS — GO HOME!'

January 3, 1983

96

'I'M FROM THE LEGAL SERVICES CORPORATION — WORD HAS IT YOU'RE IN NEED OF A LAWYER...'

January 7, 1983

'CHARLENE, THE FEDERAL TEENAGE CONTRACEPTIVE POLICE SAY YOU'VE BEEN INQUIRING ABOUT BIRTH CONTROL— NOT THAT AWFUL DEPO-PROVERA, I HOPE!'

January 16, 1983

103

January 19, 1983

'...SO YOU SEE, THE ENTIRE FUTURE OF THE INTERNATIONAL FINANCIAL SYSTEM HINGES ON YOUR CAPACITY FOR QUICK RECOVERY AND VAST ECONOMIC GROWTH.'

'LOOK AT YOU! ALL YOU INDIANS DO IS HANG AROUND THE RESERVATION. WHY DON'T YOU GO OUT AND GET A JOB?'

'OBSERVE HOW THIS ELEVATION IMPROVES THE VIEW.'

January 26, 1983

January 27, 1983

LET CUSTER BE CUSTER

111

'NATURALLY, WE ABHOR THIS SENSELESS VIOLENCE. BUT IF THOSE OTHER TRUCKERS WOULD JOIN OUR STRIKE, IT WOULDN'T HAPPEN!'

'ARISE, SIR DUMP!'

'SHARON? SHARON WHO?'

'WHEEEE!'

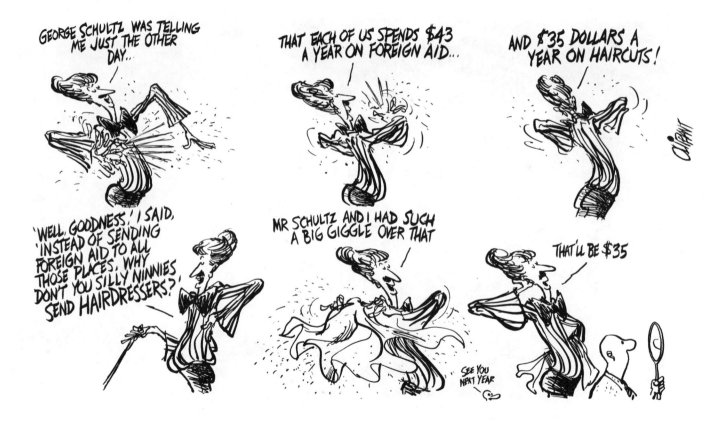

WARNING: THE ATTORNEY GENERAL HAS DETERMINED THAT SUSPECTED POSSESSION OF TICKETS TO MOVIES CRITICAL OF ACID RAIN AND NUCLEAR WAR, MAY BE HAZARDOUS TO YOUR HEALTH.

March 3, 1983

'BEATS ME — SHE WAS RIGHT HERE A MOMENT AGO!'

128

March 4, 1983

129

'A FLOWER! A SYMBOLIC DANCE TO SPRING! A LIKENING OF ECONOMIC RESURGENCE TO FLOWERS AWAKENING FROM THE DARK WINTER, THE TRIUMPH OF SUPPLY-SIDE VERITIES. IT'S PROBABLY A TRICK!'

'THAT SHOULD HOLD 'EM FOR A BIT!'

'DON'T BUST A GUT OVER IT — JUST CLEAN IT UP ENOUGH FOR RESALE.'

March 24, 1983

March 24, 1983

141

March 28, 1983

142

'NOW, WHO GETS THE COQ AU VIN, AND WHO GETS THE CHICKEN CACCIATORE?'

'SUCH A FALSE, VILE, BASE, MALICIOUS, DEFAMATORY SLANDER, MONSIEUR! WHAT COOKIES?'

'REAL AMERICANS MUST BE PROTECTED FROM THE SCUMMIER ELEMENT!'

April 12, 1983

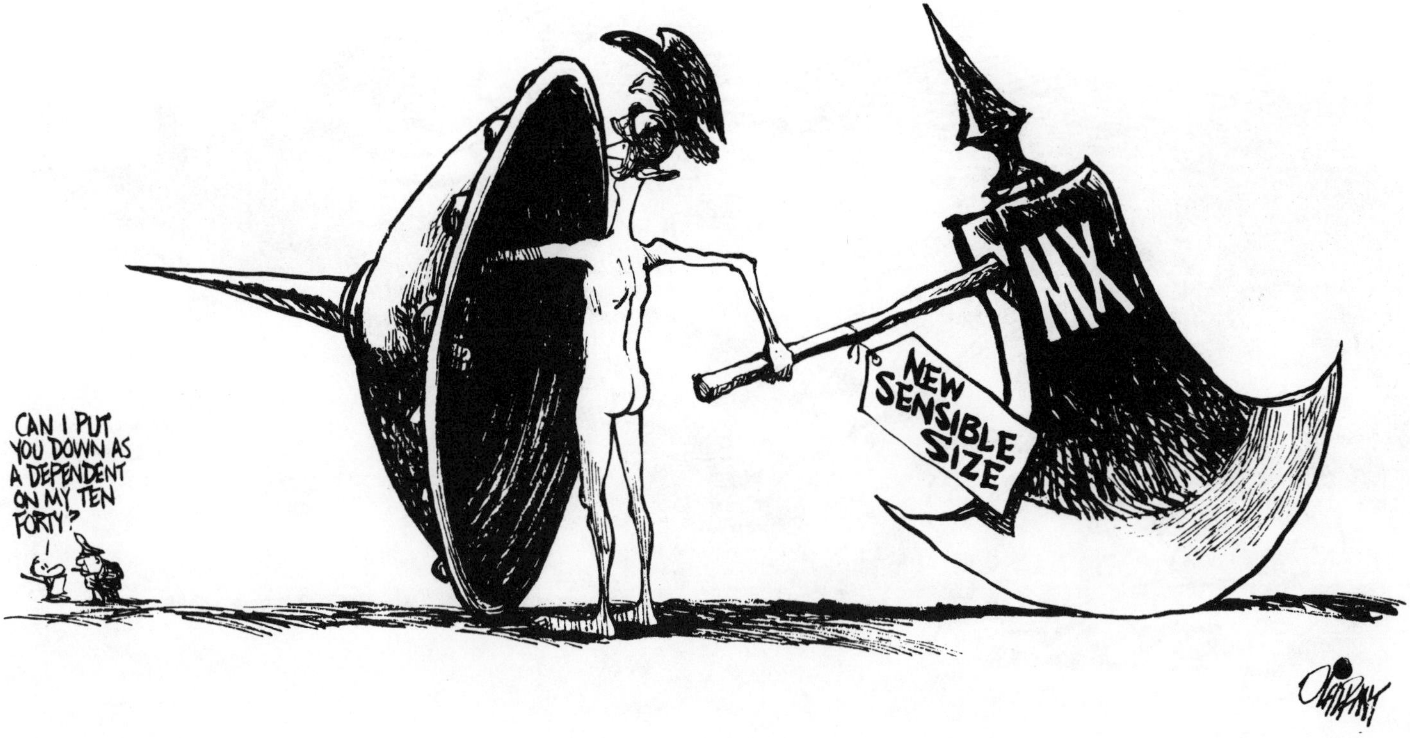

THE BATTLE FOR THE PRESIDENT'S MIND

THE WINDOW OF VULNERABILITY

'I WILL RUN AN OPEN, HONEST ADMINISTRATION.' SAID MR. PRESSER...

'WE KNOW YOU'RE IN THERE, SIR—THROW OUT YOUR CREDENTIALS AND COME OUT WITH YOUR HANDS UP!'

April 27, 1983

'YOU'RE OBVIOUSLY SUFFERING FROM AN ACUTE MILITARY AID DEFICIENCY!'

THE BISHOPS DRAFT A LETTER

ENVIRONMENTAL GROUPS HAVE MADE EXCITED SIGHTINGS RECENTLY OF THE RARE GREAT CRESTED VARI-HUED RUCKELSHAUS (OR LAWYERBIRD)

OTHER SIGHTINGS OF THIS IMPRESSIVE CREATURE HAVE BEEN MADE IN THE WEYERHAEUSER FOREST.

THIS BIRD SINGS MOST BEAUTIFULLY ANY TUNE YOU WANT TO HEAR, AND IS STRANGELY HAPPY IN DIRTY AIR.

IT IS POSSIBLY PREDATORY.

WHAT DOES HE DO WITH THE SHEEP?

EPA

BAA?

May 6, 1983

159

'DAM' LUCKY FOR US I WAS CARRYING MY TRUSTY URBAN HUNTING WEAPON!'

May 9, 1983

161

May 11, 1983

May 12, 1983

'MISMANAGEMENT REPORT, ANYONE?..'

163

'WELL, IT'S NOT REALLY A FIRE SALE...IT'S MORE OF A GOING-OUT-OF-BUSINESS SALE!'

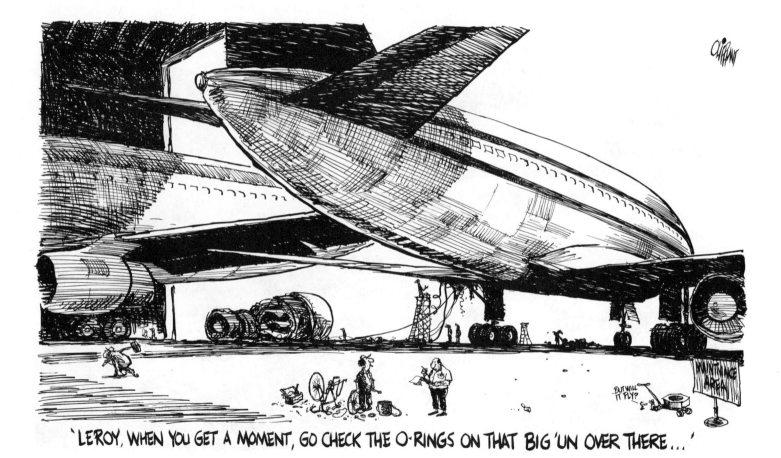

'LEROY, WHEN YOU GET A MOMENT, GO CHECK THE O·RINGS ON THAT BIG 'UN OVER THERE...'

'IT'S A GOOD SHOE, SIR, IF ONE INTENDS TO TAKE UP THE SPORT SERIOUSLY.'

'ONE...TWO...OK, WHERE'S SYRIA?'

May 23, 1983

170

'... INTO THE BACK STRETCH, IT'S GLENN AND MONDALE NECK AND NECK, TWO LENGTHS BACK TO HART...'

May 25, 1983

'THIS COUNTRY IS FALLING APART, I WARN YOU! WHY, SOON <u>EVERYONE</u> WILL BE EXPECTED TO PAY THEIR SHARE OF TAXES!'

May 26, 1983

173

'YOU CAN'T HAVE EVERYTHING, SIR — CUT-RATE FARES, GOOD MAINTENANCE....'

'YOU SHOULDA SEEN ME AT WILLIAMSBURG — URBANE, RELAXED, POISED, OBVIOUSLY WELL-PREPARED, SUAVE, DEBONAIR, WITTY, ELEGANT... WOW!'

June 1, 1983

THE ADMINISTRATION IS ADOPTING THIS MORE CLEARLY DEFINED SOUTH AMERICA POLICY.

'NOW—ER—THIS DRIVER IN HIS SEVENTIES WITH THE SHINY, BLACK HAIR, WHOM YOU SAY TRIED TO KILL YOU— WOULD YOU KNOW HIM IF YOU SAW HIM AGAIN?'

'IT IS INHERENT IN THE WESTERN CHARACTER TO HANDLE ADVERSITY WITH A BLEND OF OPTIMISM AND HUMOR — NOW, SHUT UP!'